SMOKE COLLECTION

José Moreno de la Coronilla

Introduction to slow smoking: the art of enjoying cigars and pipes

Independent Publishers Reunited

Dedicated with the warmth of a lit flame and the sweet fragrance of fine tobacco, may each of you find in your moments of contemplation a deep connection to the tradition, history, and artistry of cigars and pipes.

May every draw be a journey through centuries of wisdom, and may the unhurried ritual of slow smoking bring you joy, reflection, and an utterly immersive experience.

With respect and passion for the art of slow smoking, this dedication is for you.

Index

1. Introduction to the slow smoking world
2. History and tradition of the tobacco smoke
3. Tobacco selection and preparation
4. Choosing the perfect cigar
5. Pipe varieties and materials used
6. Lighting technique and maintaining the burn
7. The ritual of smoking: a moment of relaxation
8. The connection between slow smoking and contemplation
9. Scents and Aromas: the art of smoke tasting
10. How to properly store cigars and tobacco
11. Pipes: history, types and curiosities
12. The role of tobacco roasting in final flavor
13. Pairing tobacco with beverages
14. Cigars and culture: icons and figures linked to smoking
15. The importance of proper pipe cleaning
16. Events and festivals in the smoking world
17. The smoking and health controversy
18. The slow decline of the art of smoking in modern times
19. Stories and anecdotes about slow smoking
20. Slow smoking as an art form and social connection

Introduction

Welcome to a journey into the art of slow smoking! In this exploration, we will delve together into the rich tradition, fascinating history, and multifaceted nature of an ancient practice that goes far beyond the simple act of smoking. The art of slow smoking embraces contemplation, social connection, and personal expression through the use of cigars and pipes. Along this path, we will traverse chapters dedicated to the history and traditions of smoking, explore the selection and preparation of tobacco, examine the choice of perfect cigars and the variety of pipes, and uncover the rituals and contemplation surrounding this millennia-old practice. But it is not just about smoke—we will also discuss the health controversy, its decline in modern times, and immerse ourselves in stories and anecdotes that recount unique and memorable experiences. Finally, we will explore how slow smoking can be lived as a personal art, a social ritual, and an intergenerational bond. Whether you are a seasoned enthusiast or a curious newcomer, prepare to immerse yourself in the enchantment of the art of slow smoking. The unhurried pace of this journey will allow you to savor every nuance and fully appreciate the beauty of an experience that transcends the simple act of lighting a cigar or pipe. We are ready to embark on this fascinating journey together?

1: Introduction to the slow smoking world

Slow smoking, with its enveloping aura and timeless allure, stands as an art form intrinsic to humanity. In the silent tapestry of contemplation, smoke transcends mere act, transforming into an ancient rite that initiates reflection. Through the pages of this chapter, we will immerse ourselves in the depths of this practice, stripping away mundane simplifications to embrace its most authentic essence.

The origins of slow smoking are shrouded in the mists of time, a practice rooted in the most distant epochs of our history. From the discovery of tobacco in the Americas to its earliest traces in ancient civilizations like the Maya, smoking has traversed millennia, taking on diverse forms and meanings. What remains constant today is its ritual nature—a bridge between past and present.

In this historical exploration, we will examine how slow smoking has been adopted by cultures across the world, evolving from mere habit into a central element of ceremonies and moments of contemplation. In doing so, we will uncover how smoke has assumed profound symbolic significance, becoming a means of connection— with nature, with others, and with oneself.

Slow smoking, steeped in cultural meaning, reveals its impact not only in daily practices but in the evolution of societies.

We will explore how the ritual of smoking has helped shape social relationships, define gender roles, and weave itself into the grand narratives of culture. Through the lens of this millennia-old practice, we will analyse how smoking has become an artistic expression—a way to communicate emotions and values through the simple act of lighting a cigar or pipe.

This book will unfold through stories and anecdotes, tracing the thread of slow-smoking tradition across centuries. We will examine how this practice has endured the passage of time, adapting to different eras while remaining a constant in the lives of many. Revealing its most intimate dimension, we will also explore how slow smoking has influenced philosophical and spiritual thought, offering a refuge for contemplation in an increasingly frenetic world.

Finally, the book will conclude with a reflection on the deeper meaning of slow smoking. Through a contemporary lens, we will analyse how this age-old practice intertwines with modernity—defying the relentless rush of time and offering an opportunity to live each moment with slowness and awareness. In this journey, the reader will be invited to look beyond appearances and embrace slow smoking as an art that surpasses the mere act of lighting a cigar or pipe—revealing a world of profound meanings and human connections.

2: History and tradition of the Tobacco smoke

To fully grasp the art of slow smoking, we must delve deep into the history and traditions that have shaped tobacco consumption through the centuries. From a humble shrub native to the Americas to its global spread, tobacco carries a rich tapestry of cultural nuances and meanings that extend far beyond the simple burning of leaves.

The story begins millennia ago when indigenous peoples of the Americas first discovered tobacco. It quickly became integral to their spiritual ceremonies and daily practices. Native American cultures attributed sacred value to tobacco, considering it a divine gift and using it as a medium to communicate with the spiritual realm. This profound significance still resonates today in Native American ceremonies and spiritual practices involving tobacco.

When Christopher Columbus reached the Americas in 1492, tobacco made its European debut. Initially met with suspicion and scepticism, it gradually transformed from an exotic curiosity to one of the New World's most prized exports. European courts, in particular, embraced tobacco as an exotic luxury, giving rise to sophisticated rituals and elaborate smoking ceremonies.

Over the centuries, tobacco spread across the globe, adapting to different cultures in various forms. From the ornate pipes of Native American tribes to the elegantly rolled cigarettes of European aristocracy, tobacco became a mirror reflecting each society's traditions and preferences. The distinct varieties cultivated in different regions created unique aromas and flavors, highlighting the importance of terroir in the world of smoking.

The 18th century witnessed the birth of the first cigar factories, ushering in an era when tobacco became accessible to broader audiences. Cigars and cigarettes evolved into symbols of style and social status, while smoking became associated with romantic and adventurous ideals. In this context, slow smoking transitioned from daily practice to an act of refinement and distinction.

The 20th century brought new challenges to the tobacco world. Growing health concerns and scientific studies linked smoking to various diseases, leading to a redefinition of society's relationship with tobacco and sparking ongoing debates about its acceptability and regulation.

Today's smoking landscape features a diverse range of products alongside increasing health awareness. Yet slow smoking, steeped in history and tradition, continues to thrive as an art form that transcends the mere combustion of leaves. In this chapter, we'll explore tobacco's deep roots, examining the past to fully appreciate the wealth of meaning that characterizes the slow smoking experience.

3: Tobacco selection and preparation

At the core of slow smoking lies the meticulous care with which tobacco is selected, prepared, and presented. The choice of leaves, their processing, and the creation of unique blends are crucial elements that define the smoker's experience. In this chapter, we will explore the intricate and fascinating world of tobacco selection and preparation, unveiling the secrets behind the aromas and flavors that envelop every puff.

1. The Journey of Tobacco Leaves: The process begins in tobacco fields, where leaves are cultivated under sun and rain. The variety of tobacco, the soil in which it grows, and the regional climate all contribute to its unique character. Harvesting is done with precision, selecting only mature leaves ready for the next stage.

2. Drying and Fermentation: Once harvested, the leaves undergo a drying process, often in dedicated curing barns. This phase is essential for developing the tobacco's complex aromas and flavors. After drying, the leaves enter fermentation, where they are stacked in large piles. This carefully controlled stage stabilizes the tobacco and further enhances its sensory qualities.

3. The Art of Blending: Creating a tobacco blend is a refined craft. Masters of slow smoking artfully combine different tobacco varieties to achieve a perfect balance of aroma, taste, and burn. Blends may incorporate leaves from various regions, each contributing distinct characteristics. This selection and mixing process is a closely guarded secret, passed down through generations.

4. Tobacco Processing: Once blended, the leaves are prepared for rolling into cigars or cutting for pipe tobacco. This stage demands artisanal skill, with craftsmen who understand every nuance of the leaves they handle. The precision of rolling or cutting directly affects the tobacco's burn and the sensations it delivers to the smoker.

5. Aging and Storage: After preparation, tobacco requires careful storage. Many blends are aged for a specific period, allowing flavors to mature and harmonize. Connoisseurs prize aged tobaccos for their superior depth and complexity.

This chapter reveals the secrets behind tobacco selection and preparation, showcasing the obsessive attention to detail that true experts devote to every step. In the next chapter, we will explore how this dedication translates into selecting the perfect cigars and the diverse world of pipes—completing the circle of an art that is as much about wisdom and discernment as it is about taste and style.

4: Choosing the perfect cigar

Choosing the perfect cigar is a subtle art that requires a blend of knowledge, experience, and personal taste. This chapter will guide you through the fascinating world of cigars, exploring their varieties, shapes, and key elements that transform a simple act of smoking into an experience of refinement and pleasure.

1. The Origins of Cigars: cigars have a rich history intertwined with the traditions of indigenous peoples in the Americas. From their introduction to Europe in the 16th century to their global expansion in the following centuries, cigars have become emblems of style and status. We will explore the origins of iconic varieties—Cuban, Dominican, and Nicaraguan cigars—discovering the nuances that make each unique.

2. The Role of the Wrapper Leaf: one of the most defining features of a cigar is its wrapper leaf—the outer layer that encases the tobacco blend. Wrappers from different regions impart distinct characteristics, influencing taste, burn, and overall complexity. Varieties such as Connecticut, Habano, and Maduro each contribute their own signature touch to the cigar's profile.

3. Shapes and Cuts: Cigars come in a variety of shapes and sizes, each designed to deliver a different smoking experience.

From robustos to slender panetelas, the choice of shape affects smoke volume and flavor concentration. The cut—whether a straight guillotine, punch, or V-cut—also plays a crucial role, regulating airflow and shaping the tasting experience.

4. Fermentation and Aging: The fermentation and aging of tobacco leaves significantly enhance a cigar's quality. Cigars made with carefully fermented and aged leaves offer a broader flavor spectrum, even combustion, and greater aromatic depth. This section will examine how these processes elevate a cigar from a simple product to a work of art.

5. Pairing with Beverages: A crucial aspect of cigar enjoyment is pairing it with the right drink. A cigar's complex flavors can be accentuated or balanced by the right wine, whiskey, coffee, or tea. We'll explore classic pairings and innovative combinations, revealing how beverages can elevate the smoking experience.

6. The Art of Storage: Proper storage is essential to preserving a cigar's freshness and integrity. We'll discuss the ideal conditions—humidity levels, temperature, and storage solutions—and how meticulous care can enhance a cigar's quality over time.

Selecting the perfect cigar is a journey through history, botany, and the intricate flavors that define this cornerstone of slow smoking. In the next chapter, we'll explore another dimension of this ancient practice: the world of pipes and the art of selecting and savoring tobacco through this iconic instrument.

5: Pipe varieties and materials used

Exploring the art of slow smoking, the choice of pipe represents a fascinating chapter rich in tradition. The variety of available pipes and the materials used in their production add depth and character to this centuries-old practice. In this chapter, we will immerse ourselves in the different types of pipes and examine their constituent materials, revealing the secrets behind the creation of instruments that are far more than mere accessories.

1. Classical pipes: pipes can be divided into several categories, each with its unique style. Classic pipes include straight pipes, bent pipes, churchwardens, and billiards. Each shape offers a distinct smoking experience, influenced by the instrument's geometry, stem length, and combustion chamber size. The choice of a particular pipe type depends on personal preferences, desired aesthetics, and the intended smoking experience.

2. Traditional materials: traditional pipe-making materials have been perfected over centuries. Briar wood, commonly called briar, represents the most prized material due to its heat resistance and moisture absorption capabilities. Meerschaum, a porous mineral stone, is valued for its ability to enhance smoking smoothness. No less important is olive wood, which gives pipes a rustic yet elegant appearance.

3. Modern and innovative materials: The modern era has introduced innovative materials in pipe production. Stainless steel and aluminum offer lightweight, durable solutions, while glass and ceramics open new artistic and expressive possibilities. These alternative materials have expanded pipe design horizons while maintaining their primary function intact.

4. Artisanal production of pipes: Creating a pipe is an artisanal process requiring great mastery. Craftsmen meticulously shape each component, balancing aesthetic and functional considerations. The combustion chamber shape, stem curvature, and overall instrument balance all contribute to the quality of the smoking experience.

5. Personalizations: for many enthusiasts, the ability to customize their pipe represents a particularly rewarding aspect. Decorative inlays, special finishes, and even custom-made pieces allow transforming a simple pipe into a unique object reflecting its owner's personality. This practice has elevated pipe-making to a true art form.

In conclusion, the variety of available styles and materials adds a distinctive, personal element to the art of slow smoking. Every detail, from wood selection to stem shape, contributes to creating a unique and deeply satisfying smoking experience.

In the next chapter, we will explore lighting techniques and combustion maintenance, thus completing our investigation into how every aspect of this ancient practice has been refined to offer moments of authentic pleasure and contemplation.

6: lightning technique and maintaining the burn

Lighting a pipe or cigar constitutes an intrinsic ritual within the art of slow smoking, a practice demanding attention and skill to ensure an optimal smoking experience. This chapter will delve into the nuances of ignition techniques and fire maintenance, examining the fundamental steps that transform tobacco into a fragrant dance of smoke.

1. Preparation: Proper preparation forms the foundation of the ritual. For pipe smokers, this involves carefully filling the combustion chamber with prepared tobacco, gently compacting it to achieve ideal density. Cigar enthusiasts must first verify their cigar's tip has been evenly cut or pierced to promote uniform burning. This preliminary attention to detail sets the stage for what follows.

2. Choosing the ignition tool: The choice of ignition tool significantly influences the overall experience. Traditionalists often favor wooden matches, appreciating both the ceremonial aspect and the subtle aromatic contribution they provide. Others select gas lighters for their practicality and consistent performance. Regardless of preference, petroleum-based lighters should be avoided as they risk imparting undesirable chemical flavors to the tobacco.

3. Gradual lighting: The lighting process itself requires patience and gradual execution. By rotating the tobacco above the flame - whether pipe bowl or cigar foot - one ensures even ignition across the entire surface. Cigar aficionados pay particular attention to this step, slowly rotating the foot to establish an even burn line. The initial lighting should be treated as a ceremony rather than a hurried necessity.

4. Temperature: Following the first light, pipe smokers employ the tamping technique. Using a dedicated tool or their thumb, they gently compress the tobacco to maintain even combustion. This critical step prevents overheating while promoting optimal temperature regulation throughout the smoking session. For cigar smokers, periodic rotation of the cigar between fingers helps distribute heat evenly and prevents lopsided burning that could compromise flavor.

5. Rotating the cigar: Environmental factors demand consideration during the smoking ritual. Wind conditions may necessitate protective measures like cupping hands or seeking shelter to maintain consistent combustion. Humidity levels also require monitoring, particularly with aged tobaccos where excessive dryness or moisture can dramatically alter smoking quality. These subtle attentions separate casual smoking from true connoisseurship.

6. Winds and humidity: As the experience draws to its natural conclusion, allowing the tobacco to extinguish itself represents the final act of respect. There exists no need to smoke every last ember - doing so often generates excessive heat and unpleasant flavors. Recognizing the perfect moment to conclude forms part of the practiced art.

This mastery of ignition and combustion constitutes an art form refined through time and attention. Each step, from preparation to conclusion, contributes to transforming simple tobacco consumption into a meaningful ritual. In our next chapter, we will examine how these technical skills merge with contemplative practice to elevate slow smoking into a profound exercise in mindfulness and self-connection..

7: The ritual of smoking: a moment of relaxation

In the art of slow smoking, ritual plays a fundamental role, transforming the simple act of smoking into a moment of relaxation and contemplation. This chapter explores how ritual intertwines with the smoking experience, creating an environment conducive to self-connection and the savoring of precious pauses from life's daily frenzy.

1. Location: The choice of setting significantly contributes to the atmosphere of relaxation. Some prefer smoking in solitude, immersed in the quiet of their personal space. Others enjoy smoking in company, sharing stories and conversations over a good pipe or cigar. The selected location reflects the pursuit of a calm and unhurried ambiance.

2. Selecting the right tobacco: Tobacco selection becomes an integral part of the ritual. Choosing the right blend, the careful preparation, and the attentive handling during lighting all contribute to creating a serene beginning. This act becomes a form of self-respect, dedicating time and attention to preparing something special.

3. Lighting: Lighting the pipe or cigar transforms into a deliberate gesture, a ceremony where flame meets tobacco to create a sensory experience.

The slowness and precision of this act mark a transition, a boundary between the day's chaos and the contemplative ritual.

4. Contemplation: As smoke rises gently in the air, the phase of contemplation begins. Watching the swirling smoke becomes a meditative practice, an opportunity to shift attention from daily concerns and immerse oneself in calmness. This moment invites experiencing the present with awareness, appreciating time's slow passage.

5. Silence and deep thinking: The smoking ritual opens spaces for silence and reflection. While smoke disperses in the air, it creates precious pauses where the mind can wander, reflect, and relax. This inner silence becomes an invaluable resource, an oasis of tranquillity in an often frenetic world.

6. The ritual's goal: When the cigar burns down or the pipe goes out, the smoking ritual concludes. This final moment, observing the residual ash or touching the still-warm pipe, becomes an opportunity to close the ritual with gratitude and awareness. Slow smoking represents not just an end, but a means to achieve a relaxed and centered state of mind.

In all its facets, the ritual of smoking offers a chance to disconnect from worldly chaos and immerse oneself in an oasis of peace. In our next chapter, we will explore the profound connection between slow smoking and contemplation, revealing how this ancient practice can become a bridge to connecting with oneself and the surrounding world.

8: The connection between slow smoking and contemplation

At the heart of slow smoking lies an intimate connection with contemplation. This chapter explores how the act of smoking, in all its ritualistic slowness, can become a means to explore the depths of the mind and establish deeper connections with oneself and the surrounding world.

1. Start contemplating: The very nature of slow smoking encourages deliberate pacing. In our fast-moving world, the intentional act of lighting a pipe or cigar creates space to slow down and appreciate the present moment. This measured tempo becomes a gateway to contemplation, an invitation to explore one's inner world with calm attention.

2. Connection with senses: Slow smoking engages the senses in a synesthetic experience. The aroma of tobacco, the feel of pipe or cigar in hand, the hiss of flame - these elements combine to create a multisensory journey. Such sensory awareness builds a bridge to contemplation, allowing complete immersion in present sensations.

3. Practicing mindful presence: True contemplation requires mindful presence. As smoke drifts through the air, the smoker is called to inhabit the here and now fully.

This practice of mindfulness becomes both an antidote to mental distraction and an invitation to fully embrace the slow smoking experience.

4. Reflection and introspection: The ritual naturally creates space for reflection and introspection. While smoke curls and dissipates, the mind can wander through thoughts and memories. These quiet moments become fertile ground for exploring ideas, recollections and emotions, opening doors to contemplation that transcends surface appearances.

5. Tradition and history bonds: Contemplation through smoking also connects us to history and tradition. Lighting a pipe or cigar becomes an act linking present practice with centuries of smokers who came before. This historical dimension adds depth to contemplation, transforming slow smoking into a bridge across generations and cultures.

6. The smoke art's beauty: Slow smoking reveals itself as an art form worthy of contemplation. The craft of tobacco preparation, the blending mastery, the artisan pipe-making - all contribute beauty and meaning to the experience. Contemplation thus extends to appreciating the inherent aesthetics of this practice.

Ultimately, the bond between slow smoking and contemplation represents an inward journey through slowness, awareness and present-moment connection. In our next chapter, we'll examine how this art can transform into shared experience, revealing how individual smoking rituals can forge communal bonds among lovers of tradition and contemplative pleasure.

9: Scents and aromas: the art of smoke tasting

In the vast universe of slow smoking, the appreciation of smoke becomes a richly nuanced sensory experience. This chapter explores the art of savoring tobacco's aromas and flavors, revealing how the practice of slow smoking transforms into a true form of tasting—a journey through landscapes of unique scents and tastes.

1. The inhalation ritual: The ritual begins with deliberate, measured inhalation. This act transcends mere breathing, becoming a ceremonial opening to the tobacco's hidden secrets. Gradual inhalation allows the smoker to appreciate each layer of aroma and capture the subtle nuances released during smoking.

2. Tastes and aromas distinction: A fundamental distinction in smoke appreciation lies between aromas and flavors. Aromas are the olfactory sensations perceived through the nose, while flavors are experienced on the tongue. Recognizing this duality enriches the experience, enabling the smoker to explore a broader spectrum of gustatory and olfactory sensations.

3. Tobacco's Aromatics: Tobaccos, with their varied origins and cultivars, offer a unique palette of aromatic notes. Some may release floral bouquets, while others present woody or spicy tones.

Exploring and identifying these characteristics becomes an art form—a continuous discovery that deepens the slow smoking practice.

4. Blend's influences: The tasting experience gains further depth through consideration of blending techniques. Combinations of tobaccos from different regions and varieties create complex aromatic profiles. Each blend possesses its own personality, and tasting becomes a journey to find those that resonate most with individual preferences.

5. Cut and format effects: The cut and format of the tobacco significantly influence the tasting experience. A broad, open cut may intensify aromas, while a narrower cut can concentrate flavors. Similarly, the shape of a pipe or cigar affects smoke temperature and concentration, modulating the overall experience.

6. The retrohale: Retronasal breathing—the controlled release of smoke through the nose—represents an advanced tasting technique. This method reveals additional aromatic subtleties and amplifies the overall sensory experience. Though requiring patience and practice, it can uncover details otherwise missed by the palate alone.

7. Memorizing your senses: True smoke appreciation develops through sensory memory. Documenting personal preferences, favored blends, and specific sensations helps refine one's ability to discern and appreciate tobacco's nuances over time.

This art of smoke tasting, with its attention to detail and nuance, transforms the smoker into an explorer of the senses. In our next chapter, we will examine how the art of slow smoking can forge meaningful connections among enthusiasts, turning individual practice into shared experience and collective enjoyment.

10: How to properly store cigars and tobacco

Maintaining optimal conditions for cigars and pipe tobacco represents a crucial aspect of the slow smoking tradition. This chapter examines the essential practices for preserving these treasures, ensuring they retain their character and deliver perfect smoking experiences over time.

1. Controlled humidity: Humidity control stands as the cornerstone of proper storage. The ideal relative humidity range of 65-72% can be maintained using specialized humidification devices. This careful balance prevents the twin dangers of overdrying and excessive moisture, both of which compromise tobacco's delicate qualities.

2. Airtight recipients: Airtight storage solutions form the next critical element. Quality wooden humidors, specialized containers, or sealed jars protect contents from humidity fluctuations while shielding against external odors that might taint the tobacco's natural aromas. The container's seal must be periodically checked to ensure complete integrity.

3. Temperature stability: Temperature stability proves equally vital. Storage areas should maintain a consistent 16-20°C range, avoiding locations prone to thermal variation like cellars or garages.

Dramatic temperature swings can fundamentally alter tobacco's cellular structure and smoking properties.

4. Away from direct sunlight: Light exposure requires particular attention. Direct sunlight's ultraviolet rays degrade tobacco over time, while excessive artificial light may also cause subtle changes. Opaque storage containers or dark storage locations provide ideal protection, with cedar-lined humidors offering both light protection and beneficial aromatic qualities.

5. Periodic rotation: For collectors maintaining multiple cigars, periodic rotation ensures even aging. Moving cigars within their storage environment prevents some from becoming neglected while others receive disproportionate attention. This practice promotes uniform conditioning throughout a collection.

6. Flavor separation: Flavor isolation becomes important when storing varied tobacco types. Stronger blends may influence milder ones when stored together. Separate containers or compartmentalized storage solutions maintain each tobacco's distinctive character, particularly crucial for aromatic blends that could transfer their scents.

7. Regular inspection: Regular inspection routines help identify potential issues before they escalate.

Monthly checks should examine tobacco texture, humidification device function, and any signs of mold or pests. This preventative care safeguards valuable collections from gradual deterioration.

8. Original packaging: Original packaging often provides ideal initial storage conditions. Factory boxes and tubes are engineered to maintain proper humidity levels. Removing external plastic wraps while keeping internal packaging allows the tobacco to breathe while staying protected in personal storage systems.

By implementing these preservation techniques, enthusiasts ensure their tobacco maintains peak condition for future enjoyment. In our next exploration, we'll examine how slow smoking traditions create communal bonds among practitioners, transforming personal ritual into shared celebration.

11: Pipes: history, types and curiosities

Pipes stand as enduring icons in the art of slow smoking, carrying with them centuries of rich history and remarkable evolution. This chapter explores the fascinating origins of pipes, their diverse styles, and the unique characteristics that make them so special.

1. Remote origins: The story of pipes begins in ancient times, with pre-Columbian civilizations in the Americas crafting pipes from stone and clay for sacred rituals. When European explorers encountered these traditions, pipe smoking quickly spread across continents, adapting to different cultures and evolving into countless forms.

2. Pipe's golden age: The 17th and 18th centuries marked pipe smoking's golden age in Europe. Intricately carved meerschaum pipes, elegant briarwood designs, and sculpted human-head pipes became symbols of sophistication. This era saw an explosion of creativity, with pipes transforming from simple tools into true works of art.

3. Collectable pipes: Today, pipe collecting remains a passionate pursuit for enthusiasts worldwide. Collectors seek out rare antique pieces, artistically significant designs, and pipes made with precious materials.

Some prized specimens represent important historical periods or showcase extraordinary craftsmanship.

4. Pipes types: The variety of pipe styles offers something for every preference. Classic straight pipes provide timeless appeal, while bent pipes offer ergonomic comfort with their curved stems. The long-stemmed churchwarden delivers a cooler smoke, and more eccentric designs shaped like animals or horns add playful character to the tradition.

5. Modern and traditional materials: Traditional materials like briarwood, olive root, and meerschaum continue to be prized for their smoking qualities, while modern innovations introduce stainless steel and ceramic options. Each material affects the pipe's weight, heat distribution, and aesthetic charm in unique ways.

6. Artisanal craftmanship: The craft of pipe-making remains a living art form. Master artisans carefully shape and finish each piece by hand, creating functional objects that transcend utility to become artistic statements. These skills are often passed down through generations, preserving centuries-old techniques.

7. Fun facts about pipes: The pipe world brims with intriguing stories. Sherlock Holmes' distinctive profile was inspired by the curved calabash pipe.

Some antique pipes featured charcoal filters for smoke purification. Across cultures, pipes have symbolized wisdom, contemplation, and social connection.

This rich history and diversity demonstrate how pipes continue to evolve while honouring tradition. In our next exploration, we'll see how slow smoking with pipes builds cultural bridges, creating global communities of shared appreciation and fellowship.

12: The role of tobacco roasting in final flavor

1. Toasting as an art: The roasting of tobacco represents a fundamental process in slow smoking, profoundly shaping the final flavor profile of each leaf. This chapter examines how controlled heat application transforms tobacco's chemical composition and creates the complex aromatic spectrum cherished by connoisseurs.

2. Roasting role in the fermentation process: Roasting stands as a specialized craft within tobacco production. Master blenders carefully expose leaves to precise temperatures, catalysing chemical transformations that develop desirable flavor compounds. This delicate process requires exact timing and temperature control to achieve perfect aromatic development.

3. Roasting profiles: Closely tied to fermentation, roasting enhances the biochemical changes begun during tobacco curing. As leaves undergo controlled heating, volatile compounds emerge that define a tobacco's distinctive character. The roasting stage determines whether these compounds express floral, spicy, or earthy notes in the final product.

4. Influence on sweetness and bitterness: Different roasting profiles create markedly different smoking experiences. Light roasting preserves delicate nutty and floral undertones, while medium roasting develops richer cocoa and spice notes. Intensive roasting produces deep, robust flavors with roasted characteristics reminiscent of fine coffee or dark chocolate.

5. Roasting processes: The roasting process directly affects tobacco's sweet-bitter balance. Gentle heating maintains natural leaf sweetness, while prolonged exposure introduces pleasant bitter notes that add complexity. Master blenders manipulate this balance to create harmonious flavor profiles suited to different smoking preferences.

6. Roasting and tobacco blends: Traditional roasting methods showcase artisanal craftsmanship. Some producers employ wood-fired ovens that impart subtle smoky notes, while others use sun-curing techniques perfected over generations. Stone roasting methods create unique thermal properties that influence flavor development. These time-honoured techniques produce tobaccos with distinctive personalities.

7. Influence on the combustion chamber: In blending, roasting becomes a tool for harmonizing different tobacco varieties. Blenders may roast individual components to different levels before combining them, allowing certain characteristics to shine while softening others. This careful orchestration creates balanced blends where each tobacco complements the others.

Proper roasting significantly impacts combustion quality. Even heat application ensures consistent burning properties and optimal temperature throughout the smoking experience. Well-roasted tobacco maintains ideal moisture levels that prevent harshness while allowing full flavor expression.

This transformative process stands as a cornerstone of quality in slow smoking traditions. In our next exploration, we'll discover how these carefully crafted tobaccos become the foundation for shared experiences that connect enthusiasts across cultures and generations.

13: Pairing tobacco with beverages

The ritual of slow smoking finds its perfect complement in carefully selected beverages, creating a symphony of flavors that elevates the entire experience. This chapter explores the nuanced relationships between tobacco and drink, revealing how thoughtful pairings can enhance both elements.

1. Whisky and tobacco: Whisky and tobacco form a timeless union. A peaty single malt Scotch finds its match in an aromatic pipe tobacco or slightly sweet cigar, where the spirit's smoky depth resonates with the tobacco's richness. Conversely, sweeter bourbons may better accompany milder blends, creating a harmonious balance on the palate.

2. Coffee and tobacco: Coffee emerges as tobacco's most versatile partner. A bold espresso contrasts beautifully with sweet Virginia blends, while a smooth pour-over complements more complex English mixtures. The interaction between coffee's natural bitterness and tobacco's inherent sweetness creates a dynamic flavor exchange that evolves throughout the smoking session.

3. Wine and tobacco: Wine offers endless pairing possibilities. Full-bodied reds like Cabernet Sauvignon stand up to robust cigars, their tannic structure mirroring the tobacco's strength. Lighter white wines or aged Riojas may better suit delicate pipe tobaccos, where the wine's fruit notes can highlight the tobacco's subtle characteristics without overwhelming them.

4. Beer and tobacco: The craft beer revolution has introduced exciting new pairing dimensions. Amber ales enhance sweeter tobaccos through their caramel malt notes, while hop-forward IPAs provide a crisp counterpoint to richer blends. Experimental barrel-aged stouts can even mirror the woody notes found in aged tobaccos.

5. Spirits and tobacco: Spirits like aged rum, cognac, and Armagnac bring their own complexity to the pairing equation. A rich demerara rum amplifies caramel notes in pipe tobacco, while a dry cognac may better complement balanced cigar blends. The key lies in matching intensity levels and finding complementary flavor profiles.

6. Tea and tobacco: Tea provides perhaps the most refined pairing experience. A smoky Lapsang Souchong mirrors the earthiness of Latakia blends, while delicate white teas allow subtle Oriental tobaccos to shine. The ritual of tea preparation itself mirrors the contemplative nature of slow smoking.

7. Water and tobacco: Even simple water plays an important role. Sparkling mineral water cleanses the palate between smokes, while still water helps maintain proper hydration during extended smoking sessions. Its neutrality allows the smoker to appreciate tobacco's pure, unadulterated flavors.

These pairings represent not just flavor combinations, but opportunities for deeper sensory exploration. In our final chapter, we'll examine how slow smoking transcends individual pleasure to become a bridge for contemplation, connection and shared tradition among enthusiasts worldwide.

14: Cigars and culture: icons and figures linked to smoking

The world of slow smoking has long been intertwined with cultural history through iconic figures who embodied elegance, wisdom, or rebellion. These personalities transformed tobacco consumption into an extension of their public persona, creating enduring images that transcend time.

1. Winston Churchill: Winston Churchill's bulldog determination found perfect expression through his ever-present cigar. The British statesman's cigar became as symbolic as his V-sign gesture, representing both his contemplative nature and unshakable resolve during Britain's darkest hours. His preference for Havana cigars - consuming an estimated 300,000 in his lifetime - turned the habit into statesmanship.

2. Mark Twain: Mark Twain wove his love for cigars into his literary identity. The author of American classics like "Huckleberry Finn" famously remarked he would go to heaven for the climate but hell for the company, all while enjoying his daily cigar. His smoke rings seemed to mirror the circular wisdom in his writings, where humor and profundity danced together.

3. Sigmund Freud: Sigmund Freud's pipe became an extension of his psychoanalytic method. The father of modern psychology viewed his pipe as a thinking aid, often pausing mid-session to relight it while unravelling patients' subconscious. His collection of pipes reflected his belief that smoking enhanced "the capacity to work and concentrate."

4. **Groucho Marx:** Groucho Marx turned cigar smoking into comedic art. The quick-witted comedian wielded his cigar like a prop, punctuating jokes with exaggerated puffs that became synonymous with his anarchic humor. His cigar became as essential to his act as his painted mustache and quickfire one-liners.

5. **Al Pacino in "Scarface":** Al Pacino's Tony Montana in "Scarface" elevated the cigar into a symbol of ruthless ambition. The famous "Say hello to my little friend" scene gains additional menace from the cigar smoke swirling around the drug lord's calculating gaze, transforming tobacco into a visual metaphor for power.

6. **Che Guevara:** Che Guevara's revolutionary image remains inseparable from his cigar. The Argentine guerrilla's iconic photo - beret tilted, cigar clenched - came to represent revolutionary fervor. His preference for Cuban cigars became a political statement as much as a personal habit during the Cuban Revolution.

7. **Hugh Hefner:** Hugh Hefner's silk-robed cigar sessions epitomized Playboy's luxurious aesthetic. The magazine mogul turned smoking

into a lifestyle statement, pairing cigars with jazz and conversation in his legendary mansion gatherings that redefined modern masculinity.

8. Al Capone: Al Capone's diamond-studded cigar cases symbolized Prohibition-era excess. Chicago's most notorious gangster used premium cigars as both status symbol and business tool - his gift of expensive Havanas often preceding violent "business negotiations."

9. Arnold Schwarzenegger: Arnold Schwarzenegger's post-governorship cigar moments reveal a different side of the action hero. Whether celebrating film successes or political victories, his cigar habit represents the Austrian Oak's idea of hard-earned relaxation.

10. Ernest Hemingway: Ernest Hemingway's cigar-loving adventurer persona matched his literary style. The Nobel laureate's passion for Montecristos accompanied his safaris, deep-sea fishing, and wartime reporting, with cigar in hand as he crafted his terse, powerful prose.

11: Clint Eastwood: Clint Eastwood's cigar-chewing roles from Dirty Harry to western antiheroes created an indelible image of rugged individualism. His on-screen cigar moments - often silent, always intense - became visual shorthand for uncompromising masculinity.

These cultural figures demonstrate how slow smoking transcends mere habit to become personal signature and artistic statement. In our final exploration, we'll examine how the contemplative ritual of smoking continues to inspire creative expression across artistic disciplines today.

15: The importance of proper pipe cleaning

Proper pipe care stands as a fundamental practice in the world of slow smoking, directly influencing the quality of each smoking experience. This chapter examines the essential aspects of pipe maintenance and how regular cleaning preserves both the instrument's integrity and the tobacco's authentic flavors.

1. Preventing pipe's deterioration: Regular cleaning prevents stem deterioration by removing tar and nicotine buildup that can harden over time. These stubborn deposits, if left unattended, compromise the pipe's structure and may eventually lead to cracks or breaks. A disciplined cleaning routine maintains the stem's optimal condition and prevents long-term damage.

2. Preserving the tobacco: The preservation of tobacco's true character depends on a clean pipe. Residual deposits from previous smokes can distort the subtle aromatic profiles of different blends. Thorough cleaning ensures each tobacco variety expresses its unique characteristics without contamination from prior smoking sessions.

3. Combustion chamber maintenance: The combustion chamber requires particular attention. Accumulated residues gradually narrow this critical space, affecting airflow and combustion quality. Consistent cleaning maintains proper chamber dimensions, ensuring even burning and optimal smoke delivery throughout each session.

4. Heat reduction: Excessive heating becomes more likely in poorly maintained pipes. Thick residue layers act as insulation, causing the bowl to retain more heat than intended. Proper cleaning regulates temperature during smoking, protecting both the pipe's material and the tobacco's delicate flavors.

5. Prolonging natural life: A well-maintained pipe becomes a lifelong companion. Regular care prevents the gradual structural damage caused by residue accumulation, transforming the pipe from a simple tool into a lasting investment that delivers consistent pleasure through years of use.

6. Avoiding residual tastes: Flavor contamination poses another risk of neglected cleaning. Residual tastes from previous smokes can blend with and overpower a new tobacco's intended profile. Meticulous cleaning between uses preserves each blend's authentic character, ensuring a pure and predictable tasting experience.

7. Cleaning procedure: An effective cleaning regimen involves multiple steps: specialized brushes for stem and chamber, pipe cleaners for detailed residue removal, and careful attention to the mouthpiece.

While a thorough cleaning should follow each smoking session, lighter maintenance can be performed between smokes to maintain basic cleanliness.

This disciplined approach to pipe care ultimately serves the greater purpose of slow smoking - the full appreciation of tobacco's complexities. In our final exploration, we'll examine how these carefully maintained instruments become bridges for human connection, uniting enthusiasts through shared ritual and appreciation.

16: Events and festivals in the smoking world

The slow smoking tradition comes alive through a vibrant calendar of international gatherings that unite enthusiasts in celebration of tobacco craftsmanship. These events transform solitary enjoyment into shared experiences, offering unique opportunities to explore the depth of this centuries-old practice.

1. International cigar festival in l'Havana: The Havana Cigar Festival stands as the crown jewel of tobacco events. Each February, Cuba's capital becomes a pilgrimage site for aficionados seeking to experience premium cigars in their birthplace. The festival's highlights include factory tours, blending workshops, and the coveted Habanosommelier competition, where experts demonstrate perfect cigar and spirit pairings.

2. Chicago pipe show: Chicago's annual Pipe Show represents the largest gathering of pipe enthusiasts worldwide. This sprawling event features hundreds of exhibitors showcasing rare vintage pieces alongside contemporary masterworks. Attendees can commission custom pipes directly from renowned carvers or participate in slow smoking competitions that test both technique and appreciation.

3. Kentucky bourbon festival: Kentucky's Bourbon Festival, while primarily celebrating America's native spirit, has become an unexpected haven for cigar connoisseurs. The event's cigar lounges and pairing seminars reveal how tobacco's sweetness complements bourbon's vanilla and oak notes, creating harmonious flavor symphonies.

4. NASPC (North American society of pipe collectors): The NASPC Annual Pipe Show serves as North America's premier event for pipe collectors. This carefully organized gathering features rare historical pieces alongside innovative modern designs. Educational sessions cover diverse topics from pipe restoration to tobacco history, while the active trading area allows collectors to acquire exceptional additions to their collections.

5. Intertabac: InterTabac in Dortmund represents the tobacco industry's most comprehensive international trade fair. Professionals and enthusiasts explore advancements in pipe design, tobacco cultivation, and smoking accessories across extensive exhibition spaces. The event functions as both commercial marketplace and educational forum, showcasing developments that shape the future of slow smoking traditions.

6. New Orleans bourbon festival: New Orleans brings its unique cultural flavor to tobacco appreciation during the Bourbon Festival. The event's elegant cigar spaces, accompanied by live jazz performances, demonstrate how the city's distinctive hospitality enhances the smoking experience. Master blenders frequently introduce special editions created specifically to pair with premium American whiskeys.

7. Big smoke cigar festival: Cigar Aficionado's Big Smoke tour brings refined tobacco experiences to major U.S. cities. These sophisticated evenings combine premium cigar sampling with gourmet dining, creating environments where both newcomers and seasoned enthusiasts can explore tobacco's complexities under guidance from industry experts.

These major events represent just part of slow smoking's vibrant calendar. Regional gatherings, boutique shop tastings, and private club meetings ensure the tradition thrives at all levels of appreciation. The next chapter will examine how these experiences foster meaningful connections among enthusiasts worldwide.

The world of slow smoking boasts a diverse calendar of events and festivals that bring together enthusiasts to celebrate their shared passion. These gatherings create spaces for connection, discovery, and appreciation of tobacco traditions.

1. Cigar festivals: Cigar festivals have become global phenomena, offering structured yet convivial environments where aficionados can sample new releases, meet master blenders, and exchange tasting notes with fellow smokers. These events typically feature guided tastings, blending demonstrations, and opportunities to purchase rare and limited-edition cigars directly from manufacturers.

2. Pipe shows: Pipe shows cater specifically to the pipe smoking community, serving as marketplaces and meeting grounds for collectors and artisans alike. Attendees can examine exquisite handcrafted pipes up close, discuss carving techniques with the makers, and sometimes even commission custom pieces. Many shows include live carving demonstrations and competitions that showcase the skill and creativity of master pipe makers.

3. Food and drinks festivals: Food and drink festivals increasingly incorporate tobacco elements, recognizing the natural affinities between fine smoking and gourmet experiences. Specialized pairing sessions explore how different tobaccos interact with various spirits, wines, and foods, creating multi-sensory experiences that elevate both the smoke and the accompanying flavors.

4. Conferences and seminars: Educational conferences and seminars provide platforms for deeper learning about tobacco's cultural and historical significance.

Industry experts share insights on topics ranging from traditional cultivation methods to modern trends in pipe making, offering attendees both practical knowledge and philosophical perspectives on the slow smoking tradition.

5. Local gatherings: Local gatherings organized by smoking clubs and specialty shops foster community connections on a smaller scale. These intimate events might feature themed tastings, technique workshops, or casual smoke sessions where newcomers can learn from more experienced practitioners in a relaxed setting.

6. Whisky and tobacco festivals: Whisky and tobacco festivals have emerged as particularly popular specialized events, focusing on the natural synergy between premium spirits and fine tobacco. Master blenders and distillers often collaborate to create perfect pairings, guiding participants through the nuances of flavor interaction between carefully matched products.

7. Tobacco and craftmanship competitions: Tobacco craftsmanship competitions showcase the artistic side of the tradition, with carvers demonstrating their skills in real time and competing for recognition in various categories. These events celebrate both technical mastery and creative vision in pipe making and tobacco preparation.

Participation in these varied events allows enthusiasts to immerse themselves in the living culture of slow smoking, connecting with others who share their appreciation for tobacco's rich traditions. The next chapter will examine how these shared experiences create lasting bonds within the smoking community, transforming individual practice into collective celebration.

17: The smoking and health controversy

The practice of slow smoking exists within a complex and ongoing debate regarding its health implications. This chapter examines the multifaceted discussion surrounding tobacco use and wellbeing, presenting the various perspectives that have emerged from scientific research and cultural attitudes.

1. Negative effects: Medical research has conclusively established that tobacco smoking, including cigars and pipe tobacco, carries significant health risks. Studies link regular smoking to respiratory diseases, cardiovascular conditions, and increased cancer risks, particularly in the lungs, mouth, and throat. These findings have been consistently supported by major health organizations worldwide.

2. Nicotine assumption-related risks: Nicotine, tobacco's primary psychoactive component, presents additional concerns as an addictive substance. Its consumption affects blood pressure and cardiovascular function, while the habitual nature of smoking can create dependencies that prove challenging to overcome. These physiological effects remain present regardless of smoking method, though intensity may vary.

3. Secondhand smoke: Secondhand smoke exposure represents another well-documented public health consideration. Non-smokers in shared environments may involuntarily inhale tobacco byproducts, creating ethical questions about smoking in communal spaces. This concern has significantly influenced smoking regulations and social norms in recent decades.

4. Ongoing research: Ongoing research continues to investigate nuances within these general findings. Scientists are examining potential differences between various tobacco products, preparation methods, and consumption patterns. Some studies explore whether certain traditional tobacco varieties or artisanal production methods might present different risk profiles compared to mass-produced cigarettes.

5. Moderate consumption and risk management: Advocates of mindful smoking practices suggest that moderate, conscious consumption may mitigate some risks. They emphasize quality over quantity, proper technique, and selective tobacco choices as elements of a more considered approach. Some connoisseurs argue that the ritualistic, slower pace of traditional smoking differs fundamentally from habitual cigarette use in both practice and physiological impact.

6. Opposed positions: The debate features strongly polarized positions. Public health campaigns emphasize abstention given the well-established risks, while some cultural traditions maintain that informed adult choices should include the option of responsible tobacco enjoyment. This tension manifests in varying regulations across different societies and jurisdictions.

7. Restrictions and prohibitions: Legal restrictions on public smoking and tobacco advertising have become nearly universal, reflecting prevailing health consensus. These regulations continue to evolve, attempting to balance public health priorities with cultural traditions and personal freedoms.

This complex landscape requires individuals to make informed personal decisions weighing enjoyment against potential consequences. The following chapter will explore how slow smoking can be approached thoughtfully, with mindfulness toward both its cultural value and health considerations.

18: The slow decline of the art of smoking in modern times

In contemporary society, the ancient art of slow smoking has encountered numerous challenges that have contributed to its gradual decline. This chapter examines the complex factors reshaping this centuries-old tradition in modern times.

1. Risks knowledge: Growing health awareness represents perhaps the most significant influence. Decades of medical research and public health campaigns have illuminated tobacco's health risks, leading many to abandon or reduce smoking practices. This increased knowledge has fundamentally altered societal attitudes toward all forms of tobacco consumption.

2. Social habits and norms variations: Social norms have shifted dramatically regarding smoking acceptance. Once common in restaurants, offices and public spaces, smoking now faces widespread restrictions. These changing standards have diminished the communal aspects of slow smoking, removing traditional gathering spaces where enthusiasts could share their passion.

3. Nicotine-based alternatives: The rise of alternative nicotine products has introduced competition to traditional tobacco use.

Vaping devices and electronic cigarettes, often marketed as less harmful options, have attracted younger generations while drawing potential practitioners away from classic pipe and cigar traditions.

4. Regulation-related stress: Regulatory pressures continue reshaping the smoking landscape. Advertising restrictions, packaging requirements, and indoor smoking bans have made the practice more challenging to maintain. These regulations, while designed to protect public health, have inadvertently marginalized traditional smoking culture.

5. Cultural changes: Cultural portrayals of smoking have evolved significantly. Where tobacco once symbolized sophistication in film and literature, contemporary media more frequently associates it with negative health outcomes. This shift in representation has altered public perception, particularly among younger demographics.

6. Accelerated life's habits: Modern life's accelerated pace conflicts with slow smoking's deliberate rhythm. In an era of instant gratification and compressed schedules, the meditative ritual of preparing and enjoying a pipe or cigar struggles to compete with faster alternatives.

7. Costs growth: Economic factors present additional barriers. Rising tobacco taxes and production costs have made premium smoking products increasingly expensive. This financial burden limits access to quality tobaccos and discourages new enthusiasts from exploring the tradition.

Despite these challenges, dedicated communities continue preserving slow smoking's heritage. The following chapter will explore how contemporary practitioners adapt to these modern realities while maintaining the tradition's essence through mindful, responsible enjoyment.

19: Stories and anecdotes about slow smoking

The world of slow smoking is rich with stories and anecdotes that capture its timeless appeal. These narratives reveal how pipes and cigars have marked life's meaningful moments, becoming silent witnesses to human experiences across generations.

1. Adventurers pipes: One enduring tale tells of a nineteenth-century explorer who carried a hand-carved pipe on his journeys. Each intricate notch in the wood represented a distant land visited or challenge overcome. By campfire light, the pipe became a storytelling device, its markings prompting tales of adventure that captivated listeners.

2. Celebrational cigar: A different story recounts how a prized cigar marked career triumph. A man preserved a special cigar for years, waiting for his professional breakthrough. When promotion finally came, the shared smoke with loved ones transformed a personal victory into a communal celebration, creating a tradition for future milestones.

3. Reconciliation pipe: Cultural memory preserves the image of the reconciliation pipe. Some traditions held that sharing a pipe could mend conflicts, with the ritual of preparing and passing the pipe creating space for understanding. The shared smoke symbolized the clearing of tensions, its rising wisps representing released grievances.

4. The response cigar: Romantic lore speaks of an unconventional marriage proposal where a cigar replaced the engagement ring. When the beloved accepted by lighting the offered cigar, they began a lifelong tradition of celebrating anniversaries with the same cigar variety, each year adding new layers of meaning to the ritual.

5. Inspiration pipe: Many creative minds have found inspiration in their pipes. One writer's memoirs describe how his pipe became an essential writing companion, its rhythmic puffing helping order his thoughts. The pipe's glow in dim study light marked countless nights of literary creation, its aroma mingling with ink on paper.

6. Share cigar: Friendship too finds expression in smoking traditions. Two friends established a decades-long practice of sharing a cigar at every meeting, whether celebrating joys or weathering sorrows. Their ritual created a private language of smoke rings and shared silence that deepened their bond beyond words.

7. The wise elder's pipe: Village elders often feature in smoking lore. One account describes a wise old man whose ever-present pipe became a village landmark.

Neighbours would seek his counsel, finding that the measured pace of pipe smoking lent gravity to conversations. The pipe's steady glow seemed to mirror the thoughtful pauses in his advice.

These stories demonstrate how slow smoking transcends mere habit to become a marker of life's meaningful passages. As we look ahead, we'll explore how this ancient practice continues to adapt, preserving its essence while speaking to new generations in changing times.

20: Slow smoking as an art form and social connection

Amidst the rapid pace of modern life, slow smoking endures as both a personal art form and a meaningful social ritual. This practice offers a counterpoint to contemporary haste, creating spaces for reflection, connection and artistic expression that transcend generations.

1. Personal experience: Slow smoking becomes a canvas for personal expression, where each element - from tobacco selection to pipe choice - reflects individual taste and personality. The deliberate preparation, the careful lighting, the rhythmic pacing of each draw - these transform a simple act into a personalized performance art. Like calligraphy or tea ceremony, the beauty lies in the practitioner's unique style and attention to detail.

2. Contemplation rhythm: In our hyperconnected world, the contemplative rhythm of slow smoking creates rare islands of stillness. The ritual demands full presence - the focus required to properly light a pipe, the patience to appreciate unfolding flavors. This enforced slowness becomes meditative practice, an antidote to digital distraction and constant busyness. The rising smoke marks time differently, encouraging deeper reflection.

3. Intergenerational connections: The tradition serves as a bridge between generations. An elder sharing their prized tobacco blend with a younger enthusiast passes more than just flavor profiles - they exchange stories, techniques, and quiet companionship. These intergenerational moments preserve oral histories and create living connections to the past that no digital archive can replicate.

4. Shared time and meetings: Shared smoking creates profound social bonds. When friends gather around a pipe or pass a carefully lit cigar, they enter into a ritual older than written language. The slow, alternating rhythm of conversation and silent appreciation fosters intimacy different from typical social interactions. These smoke-filled conversations often reveal truths and forge connections that last beyond the embers' glow.

5. Social rites: Communities of practice keep the tradition vibrant. Whether in physical smoking lounges or digital forums, enthusiasts gather to exchange knowledge, compare techniques, and celebrate new discoveries. These communities become repositories of collective wisdom where novices learn from masters, and where the art continues evolving while respecting its roots.

6. Aficionados community: The craftsmanship behind smoking implements adds another artistic dimension. Master pipe carvers and cigar rollers are contemporary artisans preserving ancient skills. Their creations - whether a briar pipe with perfect grain alignment or a hand-rolled cigar with impeccable draw - represent functional art meant to be appreciated through all senses.

7. The beauty of the craftmanship: Ultimately, slow smoking persists because it answers a fundamental human need - the need for meaningful pauses, for genuine connection, and for rituals that anchor us in the present moment. In a world of increasing abstraction, it remains a tactile, sensory experience that ties us to generations past while creating space for contemporary meaning-making. The glowing ember at the pipe's bowl or cigar's tip continues to draw people together, just as fires have done since the dawn of human culture.

Conclusion

Our journey through the art of slow smoking has taken us across centuries of tradition, craftsmanship, and evolving cultural meaning. We've explored the meticulous preparation of pipes and cigars, the alchemy of tobacco selection, and the meditative rituals that transform simple smoke into meaningful experience. The glowing embers of this practice illuminate not just flavor profiles, but fundamental human needs - for contemplation, connection, and continuity.

We've confronted the complex health considerations and societal shifts that have reshaped smoking's place in modern life, acknowledging the legitimate concerns while honoring the tradition's enduring cultural value. The personal stories we've encountered reveal how this ancient practice continues to mark life's milestones - from solitary creative pursuits to communal celebrations, from quiet introspection to intergenerational bonding.

At its heart, slow smoking persists as a countercultural act in our accelerated world - a deliberate embrace of patience and presence. The careful packing of a pipe, the shared lighting of a celebratory cigar, the passing of knowledge from experienced enthusiast to curious novice - these rituals create oases of meaningful slowness.

They remind us that some pleasures cannot be rushed, some connections cannot be digitized, and some traditions retain their power to nourish the human spirit across generations.

Whether you approach this practice as seasoned connoisseur or curious observer, may these reflections illuminate slow smoking's deeper dimensions. Beyond technique or tradition lies an invitation: to pause, to savor, and to connect - with history, with others, and with oneself. In each deliberate draw, in each curling plume of smoke, there remains potential for discovery, reflection, and that most timeless of pleasures - the fully experienced present moment.

Glossary

1. **Pipe Tobacco** - Specially cultivated tobacco varieties optimized for pipe smoking, offering diverse flavor profiles and burning characteristics.

2. **Cigar Cap** - The sealed end of a cigar that requires cutting before lighting, typically applied with vegetable gum to maintain freshness.

3. **Tobacco Humidor** - A specialized storage container maintaining optimal humidity (typically 65-72%) to preserve pipe tobacco's moisture and flavor integrity.

4. **Pipe Cleaner** - A flexible bristle or fuzzy tool, often with metal or plastic components, designed to clear residue from a pipe's smoke channel and stem.

5. **Aged Tobacco** - Leaf that has undergone controlled fermentation and maturation, developing deeper, more complex flavor characteristics over time.

6. **Briar** - The prized wood from Erica arborea root used in premium pipe making, valued for its heat resistance and natural grain patterns.

7. **Smoke Ring** - The visible, concentric vapor circles formed by skilled exhaling techniques, often considered a hallmark of contemplative smoking.

8. **Tobacco Cut** - The preparation style of pipe tobacco, ranging from fine ribbon to coarse flake, significantly affecting burning rate and flavor delivery.

9. **English Blend** - A traditional pipe tobacco mixture featuring Oriental and Latakia leaves, known for its smoky, leathery characteristics without added flavorings.

10. **Drew Resistance** - The airflow dynamics of a pipe or cigar, with optimal resistance being crucial for proper combustion and flavor development.

11. **Wrapper Leaf** - The outermost tobacco leaf on a cigar, carefully selected for appearance and flavor, significantly influencing the smoking experience.

12. **Churchwarden** - A distinctive pipe style with an elongated stem, originally designed to keep smoke away from readers' eyes in medieval monasteries.

13. **Perique** - A rare, pressure-fermented tobacco from Louisiana used sparingly in blends for its peppery, fruity intensity.

14. **Box Press** - A cigar shaping method where cigars are compressed during aging, creating square edges that some believe enhance flavor concentration.

15. **Breaking In** - The careful process of carbon layer formation in a new pipe's bowl, crucial for preventing burnout and ensuring even smoking.

16. **Cold Smoke** - The technique of gently puffing to keep smoke temperature low, preserving delicate tobacco flavors often lost in hotter draws.

17. **Nubbing** - The practice of smoking a cigar down to its very end, considered either a sign of appreciation or excessive frugality depending on tradition.

18. **Tongue Bite** - The unpleasant stinging sensation caused by smoking too quickly or with improperly cured tobacco, a common novice experience.

19. **Smoking Jacket** - The traditional garment worn to protect clothing from ash and odors, now largely ceremonial but retaining nostalgic appeal.

20. **Pipe Cake** - The desirable carbon buildup inside a pipe bowl, carefully cultivated over time to protect the briar and improve smoking quality.

Author

Born amidst the fertile tobacco fields of rural Cuba, José Moreno de la Coronilla emerged as one of the world's most respected cigar authorities. His journey began in the small town where his family operated a local tabaquería, the rich aromas of aging tobacco leaves becoming the olfactory backdrop of his childhood.

From these humble beginnings, José cultivated an extraordinary palate through decades of immersive study across the world's premier tobacco regions. He apprenticed with master torcedores in Cuba's famed Vuelta Abajo district, learned traditional curing techniques in Nicaragua's Estelí valley, and studied boutique production methods in the Dominican Republic's Cibao region. This global pilgrimage gave him unparalleled insight into the subtle variations between wrapper leaves from different terroirs and the complex art of tobacco blending.

José's expertise earned him recognition as a preeminent cigar judge at international competitions. His evaluations - considering everything from combustion quality to flavor evolution - became legendary for their precision and poetic articulation of sensory experiences. Producers worldwide sought his counsel, knowing his palate could detect nuances invisible to most tasters.

Beyond judging, José authored seminal works on cigar culture. His books blend technical knowledge with cultural history, tracing tobacco's journey from indigenous ritual to modern luxury. Particularly acclaimed is his "Atlas of Smoke," which maps flavor profiles to specific growing regions with unprecedented detail.

Now a revered elder statesman of cigar culture, José dedicates himself to education through masterclasses and private tastings. His teaching emphasizes the contemplative aspects of cigar enjoyment - the importance of proper lighting rituals, the meditation of smoke rings, the social bonds forged over shared cigars.

For José, cigars represent more than luxury; they're living artifacts carrying centuries of agricultural wisdom and human connection. Whether lecturing at Havana's Escuela del Tabaco or hosting intimate tastings, his mission remains: to preserve the soul of cigar tradition while guiding new generations of aficionados toward mindful appreciation.

José Moreno de la Coronilla's legacy lies not just in his expertise, but in his ability to transform technical knowledge into profound sensory poetry - ensuring cigar culture's rich heritage continues to inspire though attending seminars and conferences all around the world

Printed in Dunstable, United Kingdom